# Visual Poems
## with
# Spiritual Messages

*Florence E. Darling*

Second Edition, 2000
Printed in the U.S.A

A personal dedication to God who inspired me to write Visual Poems with Spiritual Messages beginning June 3,1991 and I am daily being enlightened. A cherished gift for which I am most grateful and to my loving sons Scott and Shawn, whom I am very proud of.

Book Designer: Florence E. Darling

To order additional copies of this book, contact:
Xlibris Corporation
1-888-795-4274
www.Xlibris.com
Orders@Xlibris.com

# Contents

A Message For A Friend . . . . . . . . . . . . . . . . . . . 2

I Dared To Enter In . . . . . . . . . . . . . . . . . . . 4

My Sister . . . . . . . . . . . . . . . . . . . 6

A Gift From Mom . . . . . . . . . . . . . . . . . . 8

A Special Friend . . . . . . . . . . . . . . . . . . 10

My Sons . . . . . . . . . . . . . . . . . . . 12

Lovely Flower . . . . . . . . . . . . . . . . . . 14

Searching . . . . . . . . . . . . . . . . . . . 16

Little Dove . . . . . . . . . . . . . . . . . . . 18

Fooled By The World . . . . . . . . . . . . . . . . . 20

He Placed It In Your Mind . . . . . . . . . . . . . . . 22

Perfection . . . . . . . . . . . . . . . . . . . 24

Seek Me First . . . . . . . . . . . . . . . . . . . 26

Forgiveness . . . . . . . . . . . . . . . . . . . 28

I Will Answer . . . . . . . . . . . . . . . . . . . 30

I Am All . . . . . . . . . . . . . . . . . . . 32

Come To Me . . . . . . . . . . . . . . . . . . . 34

Constant Companion . . . . . . . . . . . . . . . . . 36

Weave Ourselves Together . . . . . . . . . . . . . . 38

My Touch . . . . . . . . . . . . . . . . . . . 40

Reflection . . . . . . . . . . . . . . . . . . . 42

Test Of Time . . . . . . . . . . . . . . . . . . . 44

Rebirth . . . . . . . . . . . . . . . . . . . 46

Faded Memories . . . . . . . . . . . . . . . . . . 48

I Am . . . . . . . . . . . . . . . . . . . 50

My Gracious Sister . . . . . . . . . . . . . . . . . 52

Our Hidden Glory . . . . . . . . . . . . . . . . . 54

You Have Always Had The Key . . . . . . . . . . . . . 56

Delicate Beads Of Gold . . . . . . . . . . . . . . . 58

Christmas Day . . . . . . . . . . . . . . . . . . 60

In This Place . . . . . . . . . . . . . . . . . . . 62

The Journey Home . . . . . . . . . . . . . . . . . 64

He Heard You Knock . . . . . . . . . . . . . . . . . 66

We Can See Them . . . . . . . . . . . . . . . . . 68

Stormy Sea . . . . . . . . . . . . . . . . . . . 70

My Girl "Sierra" . . . . . . . . . . . . . . . . . . 72

Unconditional Love . . . . . . . . . . . . . . . . . 74

God's Gift . . . . . . . . . . . . . . . . . . . 76

## A Message For A Friend

I arose early in the morning
With burdens on my heart,
I quickly called upon the Lord
And He took them all apart.

Together we examined them
To see those hurtful days
Then I joyfully remembered,
His kind and simple ways

So why should we concern ourselves?
With the burdens of the day
When we can hand them all to God
To swiftly take away

Our lives can be so joyous
And full of lots of fun.
Then we can look at one another
And know we're truly one.

# I Dared To Enter In

I stumbled upon my childhood
And dared to enter in.
I found the misunderstandings of life
And I locked them in a bin.

I talked and laughed with the one within,
Without ever asking why,
For in my heart, I just knew
We would never say good-bye.

I found us to be perfect,
Not a flaw did this one own.
We continued to play,
In our unique different way
And we felt very much at home

Just knowing our freedom of bondage,
Freed me from the ones who did wrong.
I chose to leave them behind me,
For I knew that's where they belong.

## My Sister

I feel so very fortunate,
To have you as my friend
Your sweetness and your kindness,
Never seems to end.

I thank myself for knowing you,
From the Spirit that's within
If we should make mistakes today,
We can begin again.

I see you as a rainbow,
Peacefully across the sky
For all to see and wonder why,
As they go passing by.

The spiritual beauty within you,
Shines just like a star.
Some will think it's something great,
That came from afar.

You yourself will know the truth
And keep it in your heart.
Until they ask for you to share
Just a little part.

Remembering the rainbow,
Your beauty never ends.
I thank God for sharing you,
As my sister and my friend.

## A Gift From Mom

Standing by her bedside,
Watching her slip away.
It's something I'll always
Remember but in a different way.

Her precious little body,
So frail and so thin,
Taught me a special lesson,
Of the Spirit that's within

The beauty of this woman,
Goes far beyond this world.
She loved the Lord and walked
With Him, since she was just a girl.

Her quiet gentle manner,
Had room for everyone.
I couldn't fully understand
"I AM" in her native tongue.
Although she showed me many times,
When I was very young.

She gave to me a special gift,
That money cannot buy.
She taught me not to look for Him,
Up there in the sky.

## A Special Friend

I found myself a special friend,
Her ways so sweet and kind
Seeing her less than beautiful,
Never crossed my mind.

She reminds me of a butterfly,
Her wings so soft and free.
The way she handles life each day,
Is not a mystery.

There's a Light aglow within her,
It cannot be put out.
For she has found the Quiet place,
We all dream about.

## My Sons

I placed my nest in the tallest tree,
So no one else could see.
I built my home on love alone,
From the One who nurtured me.

He gave me what I longed for
And He showed me what to do.
He filled my nest with the very best,
When He gave me both of you.

My sons are like eagles,
Soaring through the sky.
It didn't appear necessary,
They learn how to fly.

Their wings are strong and steady,
Not a quiver could I see.
For the knowledge of Christ within them,
Is as solid as can be.

They glided through the soft white clouds
Without the slightest sound
For they knew then, as they do now,
The Christ within they found.

He showed them how to follow
In the footsteps of His ways,
I had no cause to worry,
What a blessing in those days

## Lovely Flower

I looked into your window
And peeked into your Soul,
I saw a lovely flower,
Already did unfold.

I watched you with amazement,
To see what you would do.
When you quietly accepted,
That Christ dwells in you.

Your petals oh so beautiful,
The scent so sweet and kind
I often think about you
With beauty on my mind.

## Searching

You sailed across the waters
In search of the Holy One,
When He quietly whispered,
Your life has just begun.

You lowered the sails gently,
Then you stood there on the bow.
You had no need to struggle,
For He would show you how.

The sunset was upon you,
As you lowered the anchor deep.
You found what you were searching for,
There was no need to speak.

The seagulls perched upon the mast,
To see the lovely sight
As they watched Him transform you,
On that very night.

# Little Dove

This little dove so white and soft,
Her Soul so pure and clean
She truly is an answered prayer,
To a grandma's dream.

This little one so busy,
She has the gift of touch.
It isn't any wonder why,
She is loved so much.

The sparkle in her big blue eyes,
Oh what a lovely sight.
Gives us a clearer vision,
To focus on the Light

The cooing of this precious dove,
Is a quiet peaceful sound,
She'll gladly share with all of us,
The treasures she has found.

## Fooled By The World

My father was a gentle man
He had a heart of gold.
His worldly possessions he gave away,
To both the young and old

His body had an illness,
He was fooled by the world.
His life was in a tailspin,
It took him for a whirl.

Although within he knew the Lord,
He didn't understand.
It took him oh so many years,
To grasp on to His hand

He loved to sail the waters
And fish the ocean floor.
Until one day he gently knocked
On to our Saviors door.

## He Placed It In Your Mind

We have no cause to wander back,
Into those darkened days.
For the changes He has given us,
Are new and loving ways.

The things we thought so wonderful
We could not live with out,
We found there was a better way,
The ones He spoke about.

The days are moving quickly now,
Don't waste your precious time.
For you know how to free yourself,
He placed it in your mind.

This Light so bright and beautiful,
No one can take its place.
The time will come for each of us,
To look unto His face.

## Perfection

It was God, who breathed His breath in us,
We became a living Soul.
Many concepts, they're confusing us,
Too many stories we've been told.

To perfection we were created,
That's the way we'll always be.
The fear and disease we gave ourselves,
Do not belong to thee.

It's fear that has its way with us,
So the truth we will not know.
The past it has no hold on us,
It we choose to let it go.

To rid yourself of these old ways,
Keep watch on what you say.
Stand guard for what you really want,
For it's a new and vital way.

At the center of your being,
That's where I dwell.
The cool water that I left for you,
Are right there in the well.

## Seek Me First

We are Kings and Queens of His Majesty,
In this Royal family we are one.
We are heirs to the joy of prosperity,
Good health, freedom and fun

It's important to have the finer things,
Without a high price to pay.
Remember I said to seek Me first,
Or your treasures will rust away.

This world has a way of deceiving us,
Like the wolf that was clothed like a sheep.
The Shepherd of love watches over us,
While we appear to be asleep.

With love I gave you My only Son,
No other can compare.
So many gifts I have given you,
It would be wise for you to share.

I am the Light of a Glorious Sunrise,
In the garden of your Soul
Be still, My children and listen,
You are ready to unfold.

# Forgiveness

If only we could forgive ourselves,
For the sorrow we have caused.
Our hearts would dance with endless steps,
That we could all applaud.

The contentment that we're looking for,
It's so easy to find.
When we listen to the words of Christ,
That's in each and every mind.

His friends they wrongly betrayed Him,
When they said they knew Him not.
They stripped Him of His garments,
Among them they cast lots.

The thorns were made into a crown
And placed onto His head.
With pain and sorrow in His heart,
Yet He forgave them for what they did.

His heavy cross He carried,
Down the long and lonely street.
As they whipped Him and they mocked Him,
And they nailed His hands and feet.

Yes He opened the gates of heaven
But that's not all He did.
He gave us the gift of contentment,
When He showed us how to forgive.

It was in His last hour,
With love for me and you
When He said, "Forgive them Father,
For they know not what they do."

# I Will Answer

The beauty that surrounds you,
It takes ones breath away.
The relationship you have with Christ,
Fulfills your heart each day.

There's a very special feeling
That whispered through your Soul.
It so gently tells the story,
We so often have been told.

We're the image and the likeness,
Of the Mighty One
The way is pure and simple,
The adventure can be fun.

You're the mountains and the pine trees,
You stand tall through the storm.
With every thought and breath you take,
It's Me in human form.

I will answer before you call Me
Still as you speak I will hear.
You're My lamb of living waters,
I will bathe away your tears.

# I Am All

The tree of life is in full bloom,
It represents your life.
Carefully nourish My every branch,
Then you'll have no need for strife.

As you look ahead into the unknown,
Fear is in your heart.
Remember the promise I made to you,
That We would never part.

Until you learn to know Me as self
And know that I am All,
My beauty will be hidden from you;
Be still you'll hear My call.

For I am the voice of silence,
Listen carefully with your ear.
My voice is as clear as the crisp morning air,
For only you to hear.

Never think that you are strong enough
To walk the path alone
It's in love that I'll have you come to Me
Together We'll share My throne.

It delights Me so to give you gifts,
You're My precious flawless pearl
For " Lo I am with you always
Even unto the end of the world."

# Come To Me

The sun peeks through the morning mist,
Stillness fills the air.
The presence of the Lord is felt,
His sweetness is everywhere.

I will show you the way to know Me,
So shall I fill your heart with love,
I will quicken your every emotion,
You'll have the patience like the dove.

Come to Me as a little child,
So I can set you free.
Quietly close the door behind you,
When you converse with Me.

Your rewards will not be honored,
If you let others see.
It's in the stillness of your Soul alone,
In secret you and Me.

## Constant Companion

Let us find a quiet place,
Alone we'll go within.
Let's clear our minds of worldly desires
When we converse with Him.

Walk with Me in your garden,
Put your trust only in Me.
For I am the One Power and Presence,
Through Me you will be set free.

Run barefoot with Me through the wild flowers,
Their sweet scent fills the air.
With Me as your Constant Companion,
There will be no room for despair.

My strength and vitality is within you,
With a Spiritual endless force
Stand firm in your time of crisis,
You'll be restored with My unlimited source.

## Weave Ourselves Together

I am your lighted candle,
Forever burning in your heart.
It can never be extinguished,
Nor will we ever part.

You're every thought of malice,
Or an unkind spoken word,
Will dim My Golden Flame of Light,
So My voice cannot be heard.

As you call forth love into your life
Love that is unselfish and pure
Old hurts and fears will fade away,
Sorrow and loneliness will be no more.

As we weave ourselves together
With My Golden Thread so fine.
"You become flesh of My flesh,
Mind of My mind."

## My Touch

The earth, God made it perfect
And everything therein.
It was man who took it upon himself
And he created sin.

Recognize Me through all My creations,
I made everything lovely and sweet.
My touch is as soft as the snowflake,
Feel it gently touch your cheek.

I placed the stars in the heavens,
For all of you to see
Each time you gaze upon a star,
Remember to think of Me.

For I am the Lord of your being,
My ways are simple and kind.
As the evening shadows quietly fall,
All your cares are left behind.

# Reflection

The river is a peaceful place,
It looks so strong and free.
Sometimes I know I hear it call,
For it's a part of me.

The pebbles on the river floor,
Endure without resist.
The white caps move with grace and ease
As if time did not exist.

There are little pools of water,
That collects around the bend.
I can see the Lord's reflection,
In ever one of them.

I bathed in the cool waters,
I was refreshed from the heat of the day
Then I noticed the Lord's reflection,
Didn't go away.

I felt peace beyond measure,
The joy I cannot explain,
His voice was strong yet gentle,
I heard Him softly call my name.

## Test Of Time

At the beginning of the path Lord,
We knelt down to pray.
You gave us clear instructions
And sent us on our way.

The path we chose was narrow
And the thorns they pierced our flesh.
We stumbled through the darkness,
Our mind in search of rest.

With our physical body weakened,
Yet our Soul untouched remained.
Only the Soul endures the test of time,
In God's love we'll forever reign.

# Rebirth

Fear not of the storms of great magnitude,
Nor of the quakes rearranging the earth.
The angels of God will be here to help,
At the time of the worlds rebirth

To prepare yourself for the coming events,
Know that only love will survive.
It isn't wise for you to concern yourself,
With the way others live their lives.

Do not be fooled by mindful thoughts
Such as, despair and doom.
Cleanse your mind of all worry and fear,
Let your love blossom in full bloom

Love God, with all of your heart,
With your mind and with all of your might
He will walk with us in the newness,
Oh, what a glorious sight.

## Faded Memories

Strip me of my earthly garments Lord
So that I might be made clean.
Fill your vessel overflowing,
Like no one has ever seen.

Let the past be faded memories,
Echoing sweet melodies.
Place your blessings now upon me,
As I come on bending knees.

Let the stillness, become a nothingness
So that the world may be shut out.
Fill me with your love and wisdom,
Cleanse my mind from fear and doubt.

I have traveled far the highway,
I am knocking on your door.
Let me drink from your Living Waters,
So I will thirst no more.

# I Am

I am the raindrops on your window,
I am the wind blowing through your hair.
I am the early morning winter frost,
I painted pictures everywhere.

I am the thunder and the lightning,
The wind and the rain
We are one in the Spirit,
In the flesh we are the same.

I am not a God of punishment,
I know only the meaning of love.
I abide in the temple of human flesh,
Not far off or up above.

I am your early morning sunrise,
I am your evening sunset.
You no longer have need to punish yourself,
I already paid your debt.

## My Gracious Sister

My sister, oh so gracious,
She has a kind and loving way.
She chose to be my sister,
On the 13th day of May

She could hear the strumming of the harps
As, the angels began to sing.
When she made her entrance,
To the earth on an angel's wing.

She's as lovely as the apple blossoms,
Blooming in the spring.
Her branches heavy laden with fruit,
Was placed before our King.

The gifts of the Spirit,
Filled her cup to the brim.
Now she sings new songs of
Praises unto only Him.

## Our Hidden Glory

We visualized that we touched His garment
In and instant our Savior did heal,
When we looked at His breathtaking beauty,
We were convinced that our vision was real.

We walked together through the valleys of sunshine
There we left our addictions in time.
We were clothed with His love and understanding,
Exchanging our nakedness for His garment so fine.

We have chosen to follow one Master,
Without effort we laid down our sword.
Upon waking we found our hidden glory,
Sheltered in the bosom of our Lord.

## You Have Always Had The Key

You could climb the highest mountain,
In search of tranquillity
Or you could look within the silent Soul,
For complete serenity.

Judge not ye one another,
Be not the first one to cast a stone.
First, remove the log from your own eye
And leave your brother's speck alone.

I taught you to live in harmony,
I gave you the key to wisdom too.
Love ye one another,
The way that I loved you.

Open up your jewel box,
You have always had the key.
Watch the flowers spring up from under your feet,
When you walk the path with Me.

## Delicate Beads Of Gold

I gazed at the waterfall in awe,
I watched the sun dance through the mist.
Delicate beads of gold swirled in the pools,
I watched them closely as they kissed.

The endless cascades of water
Appeared to have no beginning or end.
My thoughts drifted back to you my sister,
Who, I cherish as my friend.

You're majestic like the waterfall,
Its secrets remain untold.
The love of God enfolds you,
Just like His delicate beads of gold.

## Christmas Day

Soft winds blow gracefully through the grass,
As if to be ocean waves,
Small critters scurry to and fro
To prepare their winter caves.

The snow falls steadily through the night,
Covering the land with a blanket of white.
We awoke to a winter wonderland,
Oh, what a lovely sight.

We gathered around the decorative tree,
It was fitting that we should pray.
For Jesus Christ our Savior,
Was born on Christmas day.

## In This Place

Spirit spoke to my Soul
And said, follow me,
Where there are countless Souls,
Yet the Spirit is only One.

We journeyed alone to this place,
Unfamiliar to most,
Where the sunbeams reflect
Its beauty from the sun.

In this place Spirit and Soul united as One,
Leaving all memories of the past to be erased.
In this place there is love with never ending joy
And the dewdrops are sweet to the taste.

## The Journey Home

The time will come for each of us
To make the journey home
The golden path is brightly lit,
We will not be alone.

There's sweetness all around you,
You're as soft as an angel's wing.
The trumpets blast the symbols sound,
We can hear the angels sing.

Your earthly duties are finished now,
The Lord, He is well pleased.
We will watch for you on the whispering winds,
Dancing through the trees.

## He Heard You Knock

Time has passed to quickly son
You have grown into a man.
Through those years of tribulation,
You held tight our Saviors hand.

The crippling disease that brought you pain,
Will not hurt you anymore,
Your faith is strong, He heard you knock,
He opened wide the door.

## We Can See Them

We can see a choir of angels
Strumming their lovely harps
Their beautiful music,
Brings Joy to our hearts.

We can see them on a cloudy day,
We can see them in the sunshine.
It matters not where or when,
Neither the day nor the time

We can see them in the meadows,
The lakes and the streams
We can see them in the vast blue skies
And in the fields of green

We can see them in the mountains
Playing in the trees.
We can see their flowing soft white robes
Shimmering in the breeze.

## Stormy Sea

Captain of our own thoughts,
Driven by the wind.
Shattered dreams left undisturbed,
For all that could have been.

Upheaval on the stormy sea
Crashing waves onto its shore.
But ah, a silence, calm and serene,
Awaits the ocean floor.

## My Girl "Sierra"

You're my girl "Sierra"
I miss you oh so much.
Although your spirit surrounds me
I hunger that I might touch.

You had an unconditional love
Looking for acceptance from everyone.
Your, joyful little spirit
Just wanted to have fun.

You're with me every moment
You go where I go
Society cannot refuse you now
Never again can they say, no

I'll tuck your memory in my heart
Until we meet again above.
Truly, you are "my girl",
I let you go with love.

## Unconditional Love

Oh, how dark this day my Lord
Deeply wounded by life's sword.

Let it pass quickly like a storm,
Abolishing discord in exchange for reform.

Instill unconditional love in our mind;
Help us never to be unkind.

Let us forgive the way you taught us to do,
Transform us dear Lord to be more like you.

Make us a symbol of peace, like the dove,
Forever we'll abide in your eternal love.

# God's Gift

From the veranda on a hill top,
We see the rushing water flow.
The birds in song, high in the trees
Entertains us just below.

Tiny lizards frolic all around,
While the oaks shed unwanted leaves,
A tranquil place, so full of life,
God's gift to all who sees.

Instilled in all God's children
A stillness lies await,
His knowledge given freely
For all of us to take.

Gradual steps towards simplicity
Hasten the choices we undertake,
When He gathers in His harvest,
We too, will enter through the gate.